WREATH
MAKING
For All Occasions

WREATH MAKING
For All Occasions

BECCI COOMBES

WHITE OWL

AN IMPRINT OF PEN & SWORD BOOKS LTD.
YORKSHIRE - PHILADELPHIA

First published in Great Britain in 2021 by
Pen & Sword WHITE OWL
An imprint of
Pen & Sword Books Ltd
Yorkshire – Philadelphia

ISBN 9781526776907

A CIP catalogue record for this book is
available from the British Library.

Printed and bound in India by Replika Press Pvt. Ltd.
Design: Paul Wilkinson

Pen & Sword Books Limited incorporates the imprints of Atlas, Archaeology,
Aviation, Discovery, Family History, Fiction, History, Maritime, Military, Military
Classics, Politics, Select, Transport, True Crime, Air World, Frontline Publishing, Leo
Cooper, Remember When, Seaforth Publishing, The Praetorian Press, Wharncliffe
Local History, Wharncliffe Transport, Wharncliffe True Crime and White Owl.

For a complete list of Pen & Sword titles please contact:
PEN & SWORD BOOKS LIMITED
47 Church Street, Barnsley, South Yorkshire, S70 2AS, England
E-mail: enquiries@pen-and-sword.co.uk
Website: www.pen-and-sword.co.uk

Or
PEN AND SWORD BOOKS
1950 Lawrence Rd, Havertown, PA 19083, USA
E-mail: Uspen-and-sword@casematepublishers.com
Website: www.penandswordbooks.com

CONTENTS

ACKNOWLEDGEMENTS 6

INTRODUCTION 8

CHAPTER ONE   **WORKING WITH WILLOW** 14

CHAPTER TWO   **BOOKLOVER'S VALENTINE** 32

CHAPTER THREE   **SPRING BIRD'S NEST** 40

CHAPTER FOUR   **FLOTSAM AND JETSAM** 48

CHAPTER FIVE   **LOVELY LAVENDER** 62

CHAPTER SIX   **SUMMER CELEBRATION** 80

CHAPTER SEVEN   **UPCYCLED HESSIAN** 86

CHAPTER EIGHT   **POM-POM WREATH** 104

CHAPTER NINE   **COSY CROCHET** 112

CHAPTER TEN   **WINTER WONDERLAND** 122

CHAPTER ELEVEN   **WILD WILLOW WINTER WREATH WITH CINNAMON AND DRIED ORANGE** 130

CHAPTER TWELVE   **JULESTJERNE WREATH** 136

    SUPPLIERS 144

ACKNOWLEDGEMENTS

AS ANY AUTHOR will tell you, a book is not just the fruition of their work, but the collaborative product of their family and friends. Whether it is the sustenance provided – a couple of ginger biscuits left on your desk by your son, or a full and frank discussion on the best colour for pom-poms with your girlfriends, it all adds to the joy of writing.

A large portion of this book was written during lockdown, so many craft and floristry supplies (including flowers!) were difficult to obtain, if not impossible. My gratitude is due to all those who patiently listened to me brainstorm alternative solutions at length.

Special thanks are due to the Pom-Pom Squad, with whom I spent a glorious few days camping in a Sussex cow field, forcing them to tie themselves up in yarn: Lou, Angela, Dave W., Sarah, and Charlotte. Sarah also was generous enough to let me continually turn up at her door with wreaths to photograph and provided very welcome tea and assistance throughout. Elsie, Gabriella, the other Dave W., Cam, and James were the Cornwall Pom-Pom Squad and deserve thanks for a lovely week, and Philippa, Tim and Katy require a special and MASSIVE mention for keeping me inspired. Ads was kind enough to help me scavenge recycled materials from building sites, Stig provided metal coat-hangers and Dan B. helped above and beyond the call of duty by helping me cut the little wooden houses out of old bits of driftwood. Noah and Vince did nothing to help whatsoever, but as their auntie I am morally obliged to mention them in the interest of fairness.

Hazel at Castle Farm, Kent, Becky and Claire at The Flower Shop, Pulborough, and Mitch at Musgrove Willow were all so generous with their time and knowledge and I cannot thank them enough for their help. Thanks are also due to Sue and Phil for their beachcombing skills, Alex for lugging my bin-bag full of pine cones in a heavy drizzle and Tishie for her exceptional floristry skills and quiche. Dear Jane, the biggest love for getting me this gig in the first place. My mum was an absolute star, counting out literally thousands of lavender stems before they dried out, and Dan W. displayed inestimable love, support, and frankly astounding patience in listening to me witter on about the lack of adhesion on ribbon and how to make seagulls out of tin foil. Lastly, thanks to my son Wolf, 'cos I love you.

Sussex, 2020.

ABOUT THE AUTHOR

Becci spent her childhood holidays on the family farm in Denmark, and grew up with a love for all things Scandinavian. Originally she trained as an archaeologist before travelling the world and becoming a successful glass artist. She now runs **www.hyggestyle.co.uk**, an online boutique specialising in Danish and Scandinavian gifts, homewares, recipes and craft ideas. She also teaches bushcraft, foraging and survival to local schools and youth groups. She lives with her son, cat and chickens, and loves schnapps.

All photos by the author, with the exception of the large wedding willow heart (John Nicholls, jnphotography.co.uk).

INTRODUCTION

HAVE YOU EVER wondered why we festoon our homes with swathes of greenery or hang wreaths on our front doors at Christmas? The word 'wreath' actually comes from the Old English 'wrīthan', meaning to 'make into coils, plait, fasten with a cord' and its use to describe a ring or garland of flowers or vine was first recorded in the 1560s. However, archaeological and historical evidence shows the use of greenery and wreaths going back to at least classical times. Ancient Greeks presented laurel wreaths to winning athletes in the Olympics, symbolising victory and peace, and the Romans were also particularly fond of them, decorating temples, houses, chariots, priests and even emperors. The pagan midwinter festival of Yule was celebrated by bringing evergreens into the home to symbolise life during the long dark winter months, and the round shape of the wreath symbolised the continuing circle of life.

Wreaths and garlands are still a fabulous way to bring blooms and greenery into your home and utilise vertical space, or welcome friends and guests by decorating your garden gate. Once you have the knack of a few simple techniques, a quick potter round the garden or even a short walk on a winter's day will yield enough materials for you to twist together a quick wreath to display on your door or dresser. With a little imagination, many designs can be made with bits and pieces found lying around the home, and can be tailored as lovely personalised gifts. Lego, wine corks and even sweeties are all easily glued on to a cardboard ring and those brightly coloured children's clothes you are too sentimental to throw away can be snipped into sections with pinking shears and tied on to a wire base, rag-rug style.

Whatever your design, most wreaths are built on some sort of base, whether made of wire, willow or other materials and you don't need to be a trained florist to make the most beautiful creations to adorn your home. In this book we will explore many ways of designing wonderful decorations using a few basic techniques, and making the most of what nature has to offer, plus some made

with easily found craft materials. The great thing about wreath-making as a hobby is that you don't actually need a huge amount of equipment, and most items can be found either in a drawer or in the greenhouse. If you don't have access to a nearby craft shop, it is quite easy to improvise an alternative.

I have attempted to steer clear from items using too much plastic, and concentrate on either reusing commonly found materials, or foraging for sustainable sources of inspiration, particularly when looking for wreath forms. Most craft shops will offer a selection of polystyrene rings as a basis for your project. However, with the emphasis now on more sustainability and less waste, greener options such as willow, twigs, moss and straw are suggested. Working with willow and moss is particularly satisfying in that once your fresh embellishments have dried out, you can just remove them and tuck some newly picked blooms or foliage into the base to rejuvenate them.

The traditional oasis foam hitherto beloved of florists as a material for their arrangements is now falling out of favour, as it contains microplastics and does not biodegrade. The RHS (Royal Horticultural Society) has banned floral foam from all its shows, including the Chelsea Flower Show, for this reason. Materials used in this book therefore rely on a minimum of plastic, and when they are used (such as the tiny toadstools in the Pine Cone Wreath), I hope you can strip them out and reuse them for another project. I have also tried to bear in mind waste reduction when creating the projects in this book. The keen crafter will often find they have a selection of materials left over once they have purchased the necessary elements and completed their chosen project. Rather than consign them to the back of your craft cupboard, there are a few extra ideas for you to make little creations using these remnants, so what would be wasted now makes a lovely gift.

Metal rings. Available in either a flat or a three-dimensional shape, they can easily be covered in moss or straw which is then wired on. Lightweight and reusable.

Straw wreaths. Made of bundled straw (as the name suggests), they are lightweight and add a lovely Scandinavian feel to any Christmas project. Not only do they look lovely simply displayed on a door or wall, they are also easy to hang horizontally with four equal pieces of ribbon tied in a knot at the top.

Willow rings. These are relatively cheap and easy to find online, although extra-large sizes can be difficult to find; I prefer to make my own as then you can ensure they are the diameter you want. Willow withies can either be cut fresh or purchased online.

Grapevine rings. Grapevines are best harvested during their dormant season from September to April, and are very easy to twist into a wreath shape in a similar manner to willow. They are also available online and from craft shops, and have a slightly 'twiggier', scruffier appearance than willow forms, which is very well suited to rustic designs.

Cardboard rings. Suitable for lighter projects, thick cardboard can easily be cut to size using a Stanley knife. To mark out your circle, you will need a pencil, a drawing pin and a piece of string. Tie the pencil to the string, and then using the drawing pin, secure it to the cardboard so the string measures the diameter of the outside of the circle you require. Draw the circle and then repeat again for the inner measurement.

Sharp scissors. Follow my grandmother's advice and never use fabric scissors for cutting paper or you will ruin them in no time.

Secateurs. I prefer ratchet secateurs as they use much less force if you are trying to snip through a particularly tough piece of willow or twig; they are also great for cutting through thick rope when making nautical wreaths.

Wire cutters. Yes, I do occasionally cut wire with scissors, but every time I do it I think of my granny and feel guilty.

Flat-nosed pliers. Handy for pinching wire into a heart shape or straightening out coat-hangers.

Hot glue gun and sticks. Glue guns with two heat settings are preferable: the cooler setting is ideal for working with paper, whereas the higher temperature is better suited for projects where you need a bigger quantity of hotter glue flowing through, such as sticking pine cones or pom-poms.

PVA or school glue. White adhesive is perfect for those smaller items where using a hot glue gun would be verging on the risky. Also useful for gluing any fabric that you want to stiffen and then cut to shape with scissors.

Garden wire. I use a mild steel wire as it is strong but easy to bend into shape.

Floristry wire. Reel wire is particularly good as it is light and strong, and makes wiring bunches of blooms a breeze. My only caveat would be that the cut end can be surprisingly sharp, and I have suffered a number of minor finger puncture incidents when not paying sufficient attention, so do be careful.

Floristry tape. This is not sticky in the traditional sense in as much as it is designed to stick only to itself. Consisting of paper tape coated with a thin layer of wax, it is activated when stretched and warmed up by your fingers. To attach a little bunch of flowers together, start off by taping around the stems once just a few centimetres under the flower heads and fixing the tape back on to itself; now hold that point, and start to turn the bunch away from you, so the tape is effectively winding its way down the stems. Pull and stretch the tape as you go to release the glue. Finish by snipping off with scissors and sticking it back down onto itself. Be warned, you might get quite sticky! A damp tea towel kept nearby may come in useful for cleaning your fingers while working.

Hammer and nails. Useful for projects involving driftwood, and where one is making little dioramas.

Sewing thread and needles. Extra-strong cotton thread is preferable, as you are often dealing with hessian fabric or thick ribbons and you will want a fairly hefty stitch.

Wire coat-hangers. You don't seem to see these in clothes shops any more but your local dry-cleaner will have some; mine is always happy to give me a couple in return for a sausage roll. The advantage of using these as a base is that they already have a handy hanging hook, and can easily be bent into a circle or a heart with flat-nosed pliers. They also help solve that problem of how to hang your wreath without banging a nail into your front door. Stretch your coat-hanger out as far as it will go, straightening it with your pliers, then bend the tip into a square shape so it will fit over the top of your door. Twist the hook 90 degrees so it is pointing in the opposite direction. The square loop can then be hung over your door, and the wreath suspended from the hook.

If you are hanging wreaths all year round and would like a more permanent solution, fasten a coat or cup hook upside down to the interior of your front door. Your wreath can then be suspended on long ribbon which passes over the top of the door and loops round the coat hook.

Acrylic paint. Cheap and cheerful, it is also easy to clean up. Handy for painting forms in the overall colour of the design before you start attaching embellishments, just in case you don't want flashes of a brown base peeping through.

Chalk paint. Not all chalk paints are created equal! I have a particular fondness for Rustoleum Chalky Finish Furniture Paint in Chalk White. Not only does it clean up beautifully (from both brushes and spillages), it has excellent adhesion to both wood and metal. You can mix it with acrylic paint to achieve the colours you want, and best of all, as the paint starts to thicken up and run out, you can easily add a little more water to extend its life further.

An old toothbrush. I find toothbrushes much easier for painting anything with stiff spines or bristles, when you want to add a snowy effect rather than overall coverage.

At least one decent small paintbrush. Obviously cheap paint brushes are fine for most projects, but I would suggest owning at least one good quality brush from the art shop for adding tiny details to embellishments, as it will carry the paint better.

CHAPTER ONE

WORKING WITH WILLOW

WILLOW IS A FANTASTIC resource for the keen wreath maker; not only is it very versatile for creating wreaths and basketry but it also has superb eco-credentials over more artificial materials such as polystyrene and oasis foam. Traditionally grown in the wetlands of Somerset, owing to its deep and boggy peat beds, it can easily be found growing by water or damp footpaths, and is best cut between December and March (this is known as green willow), when the leaves have fallen. Bring freshly cut green willow indoors for a few hours to warm up before you start to work with it, as this will make it more flexible.

The rest of the year you can either cut the withies and strip the leaves off, or work with dried, or brown willow. Easily available online and cheaply purchased in bulk, it comes in various lengths which are measured in feet, and sold by weight. A wreath made with five or six 7ft withies will give you a lovely round form of roughly 30cm. However, before you begin working with your brown willow, it will first need to be soaked in order to render it flexible.

A rough rule of thumb is that it needs to be steeped one day for every foot of its length; hence a 6ft willow will need soaking for six days. Rather than soaking your brown withies in the bath (which not only renders it unusable for other family members during this period but can also stain it quite badly), I would suggest using a soaking bag, also available from willow suppliers. You simply put the willow into the bag, half fill it with water and then fold the top over and secure with pegs or freezer bag clips to make sure the water doesn't leak out. Turn the bag over twice a day so the withies soak evenly, and leave for the appropriate number of days. Drain the water out and leave the willow in the bag overnight; it is then ready to use. You can test whether the willow is ready to use by winding the thickest part around your hand; it should bend easily and not crack or split.

Wreaths need not always be round! Hearts are always popular symbols of love and celebration, and are easily created with just a few withies or bendy twigs, some secateurs and either reel wire or raffia to bind the joins. Stars are even easier to make and are slightly more robust, so well suited to blustery front doors and gardens.

CIRCULAR WILLOW WREATH

1. To make a basic willow form, take one of your withies, hold the butt end in your left hand and bend it round into a loop.

2. Wind the tip around the back and then weave it round and round the form, heading to the right. Tuck the end in to secure.

3. Turn your wreath roughly 60 degrees to the left, and repeat; stick the butt end in from front to back towards the left, leaving a little tail sticking out, then continue to wrap the tip around until you can go no further. At this point you might be starting to worry slightly that your beautiful wreath has a scruffy egg shape, but don't panic; keep turning the wreath to the left, inserting a new butt, and then winding the tip to the right.

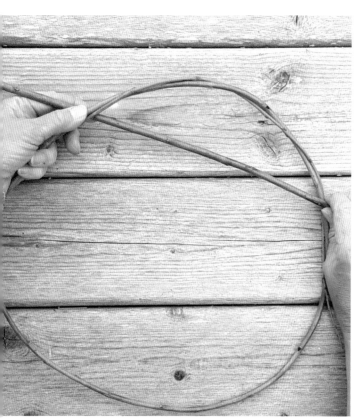

4. After you have woven in six withies, you should be back roughly where you started.

5. Now you can apply a little pressure where needed, gently easing the willow into a circular shape. When you are happy with it, snip the butts and tips off, always holding your secateurs at the same angle to make it look neat.

SIMPLE WILLOW HEART

1. Select two bundles of three long withies, soaked if necessary. Gently bend each bunch into a U-shape, working along the length slowly to avoid the risk of snapping them.

2. Form the thicker ends of the two bunches into an X-shape and secure with reel wire or raffia.

3. Now bend in both the U-shapes until the mid-sections cross each other and form a heart shape, with the tips sticking out past the far edge of the other bundle.

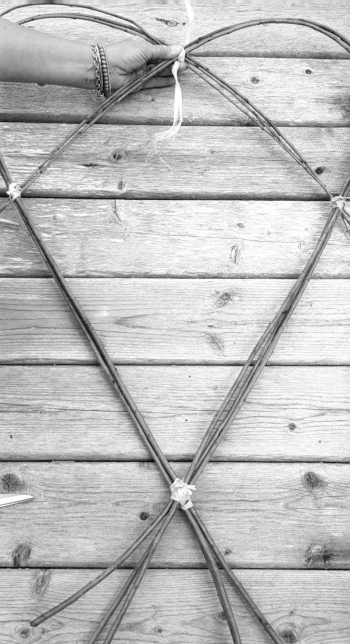

4. Tie in place with wire where they form a cross at the top, then wrap more wire or raffia around the other joins.

5. Wrap all the crossing points with raffia to add strength and cover the joins, and then trim off the ends.

6. Take a 6-inch section of wire and fold in half to make a hanging loop. Twist the ends around each other a few times, then put the loop behind the wreath at the top of the heart, and wind the tails around the willow a couple of times to secure. Leave plain or tuck in a few flowers and some honeysuckle for an instant touch of summer.

WILLOW STAR WREATH

1. Cut your willow withies into twelve 45cm lengths using secateurs (this will give you a finished diameter of about 50cm).

2. Lay them out in pairs and arrange three bundles into a triangle, crossing them over about 5cm from the end.

3. Secure each join by wrapping with raffia and tying the ends. Snip off any excess.

4. Repeat with the other three bundles to make a second triangle.

5. Lay the triangles on top of each other to make a star shape, and wire or tie them together where they cross. Trim the ends with secateurs to neaten them up, then hang with a raffia bow to finish.

STAR POT STICK

These sweet little stars can be made in a matter of moments; leave the stem long and use the star as pot stick, or trim off the excess and use as an embellishment on a Christmas wreath or on your tree. It would also make a great magic wand for your little witches at Halloween.

1. Take a withy and holding it by the butt, bend it an angle to the right, about a third of the way along.

2. Working with the long end, bend it again at about 15cm along, back over the main stem.

3. Bend again at about 20cm, crossing behind the main stem. Push it through the body of the star from the back to the front.

4. Lastly, bend again at about 20cm, bringing it back behind the star. Wind the tip down the stem and tuck the tip into one of the wraps to secure then leave to dry.

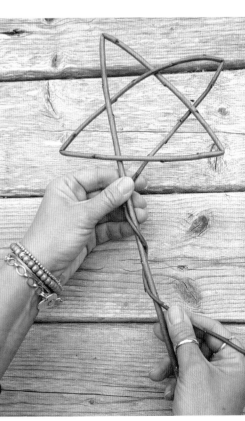

WILLOW BALLS

Willow balls are very versatile; use them to add an extra three-dimensional aspect to your wreaths, or fill full of battery fairy lights to brighten up a dull corner. They look wonderful grouped on a dresser or your Christmas table, wound round with a little ivy, and you can even use them as rustic bird feeder; simply suspend on some jute string and pop a couple of fat balls through the twigs.

1. Take a willow withy (soaked if necessary); if it is freshly cut, strip off any extra leaves.

2. Form a circle the same diameter as you wish the ball to be, then wind both ends around to form a ring.

3. Trim off any excess and repeat with three more withies to form three more rings roughly the same size.

4. Now take one ring and push it into the other to form an X-shape, giving you the base of the ball, then push on the other two wreaths to make it spherical.

5. Insert another withy between two of the twists on the existing rings, winding it in and out of the sphere.

6. Finish it off by tucking the tip and the butt securely in between a nice tight gap, then snip off any excess. Repeat until the ball is covered.

WILLOW PLANT CLIMBER

If you have ordered your willow withies in bulk online, you will inevitably find you have some left over after making your wreaths; what better way to use them up than this lovely garden obelisk? These are perfect for growing both sweet and garden peas, as they utilise valuable garden space and encourage the plants to grow vertically so they don't trail along the ground and rot. If you do not have a suitable log available to use as a frame, any round marker to give you a rough outline will do. Place a dustbin lid on a soft lawn, and then push the willow evenly around the edge to give you a circular shape.

MATERIALS

- Brown willow withies, soaked (I used 6ft ones for this project)
- Secateurs
- String
- A round section of log
- A drill and a bit that corresponds with the diameter of your willow. For this piece I used a 8.5mm drill bit, as it held the willow snugly but I was still able to remove it at the end.

1. Decide how large you would like the base of the obelisk to be, then draw a circle on your wooden log to that size. (The easiest way to draw the circle is by hammering a nail into the centre of the log, then tying a pencil to it, to use as a compass.)

2. Once you have marked out the log, decide how many uprights you would like your obelisk to have, then drill a corresponding number around the circle, spaced evenly apart. Make sure you have an odd number.

3. Insert a withy into each of the holes.

4. Tie some string loosely round the tips of the willow, just to give you a better idea of the final shape.

5. Starting about 20cm up from the bottom, insert a withy butt between two uprights, and begin to weave the willow in and out.

6. Always add the butt pointing in the same direction as the last one as it will give you a more even finish; I tend to insert the butt from right to left and front to back, whatever project I am working on, then I weave the tip towards the right.

7. Once your working section has reached a decent width of around 10cm, trim off any excess, and repeat the woven band twice more, angling the uprights gently inwards as you move upwards.

8. Tie a couple of smaller flexible withies around the top to finish the structure, and remove the string.

9. Gently pull the obelisk out of the log base, and trim all the ends to the same length with your secateurs, ensuring you leave enough to push into the pot or flowerbed.

10. Once you have mastered the basic technique, you can add a little extra flourish; adding two more withies circling the frame between bands adds a lovely touch of movement.

QUICK GARDEN WREATH

This little summer wreath was made on a lovely Sunday afternoon in early summer, after a friend brought round a beautiful bunch of hydrangeas as a gift. I cut six willow withies from the garden, leaving the leaves on to act as a green background and provide some mass, and then wove them into a quick and basic circle. Hydrangea is fabulous for projects like this as it has thick and flexible stems which are very forgiving, so I just tucked them in between the willow twists. We also appeared to have a burgeoning glut of apples, but the little fruit have an alarming (and annoying) habit of dropping off their stems while you are working with them, so I pushed a 20cm section of wire through the base of each apple and twisted the ends together. They were then simple to attach to the wreath, nestled in between the hydrangea blooms.

Any wreath made without a water source (such as oasis foam), is going to dry out very quickly, but I think that the glorious thing about this arrangement is that as the flowers and foliage dry it adds an extra dimension to the overall effect. As the apples started to get a touch squishy, I stripped them out and added some lavender instead. This added a little height and contrast to the delicate dried hydrangea petals.

Green willow rings look wonderful for a wedding or garden party. Follow the instructions as above, but leave the silvery leaves on for a wild and rustic feel. This huge summer wreath was the result of a (slight) miscommunication regarding a friend's wedding. The beautiful bride had requested a willow heart to decorate the side of a Sussex barn, imagining it would be a couple of feet in diameter. I, on the other hand, thought it was supposed to be as big as a figurative barn door, and made one that was over 8 feet high, which had to be wrestled into place on a terribly hot day by some very kind gentlemen with ladders.

CHAPTER TWO

BOOKLOVER'S VALENTINE

EVEN AS I TYPE, I am surrounded by piles and piles of books which I am too sentimental to send to the charity shop. In addition, I have an appalling memory and can read the same book twice within the space of a couple of months; never am I able to remember the ending, so I am always loath to get rid of them in case I fancy something 'new' to read.

This wreath therefore is the perfect way to recycle that paperback that has too many coffee stains to send to the charity shop but still holds a special place in your heart. A wonderful gift for the bibliophile in your life, it also looks fabulous when made with old sheet music and would make a great addition to a vintage-style wedding or Valentine's dinner. I have used very simple paper roses in the heart design shown in the main photograph, but if you wish to have larger flowers, follow the instructions to make the six-part roses. Cutting three or four pages into a spiral at once will also save you lots of time.

Here we are using a wire wreath form, and wrapping it with reel wire before starting to affix the embellishments. This technique is very handy as although wire forms come in a wide selection of shapes and sizes, it is not always that easy to glue things to them. Adding wraps of wire provides a little more surface area with which to work.

MATERIALS

- An old paperback book
- 30cm wire heart wreath
- Reel wire
- Scissors
- Glue gun and glue sticks
- Wire cutters
- 80cm natural raffia or ribbon

1. Prepare your form. Tie one end of your reel wire on to the wire wreath and wrap it all the way around, pulling it tightly as you go.

2. Wind the end a couple of times around the wreath once you have returned to the beginning, and snip off.

3. Heat up your glue gun and add some blobs of glue at both the inside and outside edges, where the wreath and the reel wire intersect; a blob every 3cm should be plenty.

4. Tie your ribbon or raffia on to the top of the heart to make your hanging loop.

5. Carefully pull some of the pages out of your paperback and cut them into a square (this will be roughly 10cm x 10cm for your average airport thriller).

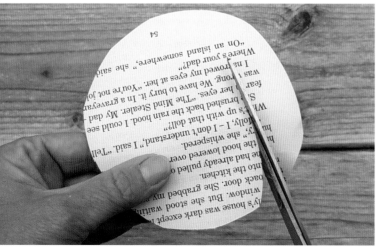

6. Round off the corners to give you a circle.

7. Now starting at the edge, cut your circle into a spiral; I find that a width of 2cm will give you between two and three revolutions as it were. Leave a small round tab in the centre as this will be the base of the rose.

8. Starting at the outside edge, roll the

paper tightly towards so you, turning the spiral as you go so that the paper takes on a cone shape.

9. When you reach the centre of the spiral, continue to hold the paper so it stays rolled up, then apply a generous squirt of glue to the central tab. Push the roll into the glue, just easing up the pressure a little bit so the rose unfurls slightly.

10. Pull the glue gun away, letting a small amount of adhesive trail along the remaining area of tab, then fold this up so it holds everything in place.

11. Repeat until you have eighty or so roses (although I would suggest make a couple of extra spare ones).

12. Glue the roses on the frame. I find that if you start sticking them on along one of the long sides, two roses will fit side by side quite neatly, then you can add extra ones in at the bends to fill the extra space.

To make roses with individual petals, you will need a paperback book, scissors, a glue gun and a wooden cocktail stick. These lovely flowers can also be made into a bouquet; when you are cutting the rounded top off the triangle, cut a tiny snip from the bottom as well, to make a hole in the middle. When the rose is assembled, simply slide a piece of wire into the hole at the base of the rose and glue in place to make a stem.

1. Cut three 10 x 10cm squares from your book.

2. Fold each square in half, then repeat twice more so you have a neat little triangle.

3. Cut the wide edge of each triangle into a rounded shape. At this stage you can add a little touch of colour to the rose by applying a good healthy dose of felt tip to the cut edge.

4. Cut one petal out of one of the shapes, two petals out of the next and three out of the last one. Keep these sections safe.

5. Take the six-petal piece and apply glue to the last section. Fold it round and stick it to the first section so you have a cone shape.

6. Repeat this process with the five-, four-, three- and two-petal pieces.

7. Roll the one-petal piece into a tight cone and secure with glue.

8. Taking the six-petal piece, roll the edge of each petal around the cocktail stick to give it a curled edge.

9. Repeat this process with all the other pieces except the rolled cone.

10. Now you can assemble the rose. Apply some glue to the outside of the smallest piece and then push it into the centre of the next one up in size, holding it in place until the glue has set. Repeat with the other pieces, alternating the petals so the rounded edges are staggered between the layers.

CHAPTER THREE

SPRING BIRD'S NEST

EVERY HEART MUST surely be gladdened by the first sights of spring, with tiny shoots of life popping forth here, there and everywhere. This lovely wreath features hand-painted wooden eggs nestled on to a willow ring, with padded fabric birds providing a welcome burst of vibrant colour after the grey days of winter. Twist a little green foliage around the willow once you have completed weaving the form to bring in a touch of the fresh outdoors. I think it is pretty enough not just for Easter, but to see you all the way through to early summer.

Plastic or polystyrene eggs are available at many craft shops, but I think it is worthwhile searching for wooden ones, not just for environmental reasons but also practical ones. The plastic versions are an absolute nightmare to paint as even acrylic paint tends to slip straight off, and it can be difficult to make glue adhere. If it is too early for Easter and you have problems sourcing wooden eggs, you can always make a fairly decent version with water balloons. Blow up the balloons until they are 4 or 5cm in length, and then apply alternating coats of tissue paper (or even loo roll) and PVA glue, leaving the 'tail' poking out. Once they are dry, pop the balloons and remove their deflated skins through the hole, gluing on a couple more squares of tissue to cover the gaps.

The little birds are perfect for using up any scraps of cotton fabric you have left over from other projects, or you can purchase a pack of fat squares (pre-cut squares of material designed for quilt making) in coordinating designs. Instead of using polyester toy filler, you could also stuff them with hamster bedding; not only is this sold in much smaller bags, making it an economical alternative, it is also made of plant fibres rather than a plastic derivative.

Other materials for this project were found in the garden and out on a country walk; honeysuckle is perfect for winding round forms

and adding a little 'twigginess' as it is so flexible, and if fresh foliage is not available, green satin leaf trim is readily available online or at most haberdashers by the metre.

MATERIALS

One 45cm willow wreath (after weaving it I applied pressure to either side to give it a more oval egg shape)

- 2m honeysuckle, or other flexible branches
- Twelve 4cm wooden eggs (if they are designed to be hung for Easter, just snip off the loop and sand down if necessary)
- One bunch of silk flowers (I used yellow narcissi)
- Cotton fabric in spring colours
- 2m of green leaf trim
- Natural raffia
- Feathers
- Needle and thread
- Toy stuffing or hamster bedding
- Four empty loo roll tubes
- White chalk paint
- Coloured acrylic paints
- Paintbrushes
- Old toothbrush
- Reel wire
- Hot glue gun and glue

1. Cut each of your loo roll tubes into three, to act as little stands for your eggs while they dry.

2. Prepare your eggs. Snip off any hanging loops and sand flat. Paint with a layer of white chalk paint, as this will make your final design seem brighter.

3. Allow to dry and then add your design. If your fabric birds have quite a busy pattern, the eggs will look wonderful if just painted in two or three different shades, to add a plainer contrast.

4. Once they are dry, mix up some white chalk paint with an equal amount of water and stir well. Dip your toothbrush in the paint and shake off any excess.

Hold the brush above your eggs and flick the paint on with your thumb, creating a fine splattered effect.

5. Add a touch of black acrylic paint to your mixture to make grey and stir well. Flick this on as well, to add a little texture.

6. If you would like a more folk art feel, paint a broad stripe of paint around the mid-section of the egg, allow to dry and then add little dotted flowers. I find the easiest way to do this is by turning the paintbrush upside down and using the tip of the handle, as this gives you a lovely round blob of paint. The blunt end of a wooden kebab stick also works well. Leave the eggs on your loo roll stands so they don't roll around the table when wet, thus smudging all your hard work.

7. To make the little birds, photocopy or sketch out the bird pattern supplied at the end of the book. Place two pieces of your chosen fabric right sides together, draw round the pattern and cut out. Hand or machine stitch round the design, leaving a 3cm gap along the long edge of the bird's tummy. Turn the material inside out, poking

the beak out into shape with the end of a paintbrush. Stuff with toy stuffing or hamster bedding and stitch neatly shut.

8. Repeat with your other fabric scraps until you have five little birds.

9. To make the wings, cut the pattern out of thin card. Work out which way you would like the wing pointing to suit your design, then paint on a generous layer of PVA and glue the fabric on right-side up.

10. Once the glue has dried, trim the fabric round the wing, leaving a 1cm border. Make little snips with your scissors right up to the card, to create small tabs.

11. Add another layer of glue and fold the fabric tabs in. As it dries, the card may contract a little, but I think this adds a lovely shape to the wing.

12. Heat up your hot glue gun and attach the wings to the birds.

13. Take four or five 80cm lengths of raffia and bunch them together. Pass them through the hole in the wreath and knot at the top, to make the hanging loop.

14. Wind your honeysuckle around the wreath, adding in more sections and securing with a twist of reel wire if necessary.

15. Now add your leaf trim. Rather than winding it round and round in an organised way, I draped it in and out of the twigs to give a slightly more organic feel, adding a few blobs of glue here and there to secure.

16. Attach the birds to the wreath. The easiest way to do this is by squeezing a large blob of glue on to the back of each bird, and holding it firmly on to the form until the adhesive hardens. Squirt a little more glue in the join if necessary. Try and tuck one or two of them in between the honeysuckle branches to make it appear as if they are perching.

17. Glue on the eggs, spaced around the wreath in groups of two or three. Once again it is easiest to apply the glue to the egg, pressing it firmly down on the wreath until the adhesive hardens. Squirt more in from the side if necessary.

18. Tuck the little feathers in around the eggs to make nests, securing them with a tiny blob of glue.

19. Split your bunch of silk flowers into sprigs (they usually come apart quite easily), and glue each sprig on to the form, tucking the stem down in between the branches.

20. Tidy up any loose strings of glue (the hot glue gun tends to make little cobwebby trails), then take five or six 80cm lengths of raffia and tie a bow around the bottom of the hanging loop. Fix the bow in place with a blob of adhesive and trim the ends.

HOW TO MAKE A CREPE PAPER GARLAND

If you cannot source either fresh foliage or leaf trim, you can make your own pretty leaf garland from crepe paper. The easiest way to make this requires a sewing machine. I would say, however, that any wreath that includes crepe paper will not be weatherproof; one drop of liquid (be it wine or coffee) will cause an irreparable mark, so they are best kept indoors.

1. Cut leaf shapes out of crepe paper, with the grain going down the length of the leaf.

2. Using a variety of sizes and colours to add texture, cross a couple of leaves over at the base and sew down vertically.

3. Continue to feed in a variety of colours and sizes, stitching them together on your trusty machine, and ensuring you cross the tip of each new leaf over your mid line.

CHAPTER FOUR

FLOTSAM AND JETSAM

BEACHCOMBING IS ONE of our family's favourite activities, even in the most wintry and wet of conditions, and I don't think we have ever returned from a beach trip without a car boot filled with 'things that might come in useful'. I still remember my son, then aged 8, finding a huge and fairly odorous catch box that must have washed overboard from a fishing trawler. Dragging it along a 600m stretch of shingle in the January drizzle 'because it would be handy for toys', he insisted on filling it up with more and more large stones as we walked along. By the time we got back to the car he had slowed to a soggy but obstinate crawl. Four years on, it is still waiting in the garden.

Last Christmas we made lots of little beach hut dioramas from all of this gathered flotsam to give to family and friends as gifts. They worked surprisingly well, so I thought it might be fun to try and make a diorama into a wreath, so it wouldn't take up so much valuable space on my cluttered dresser. The example featured is merely an inspiration for you to customise as you see fit, with the materials you have foraged. I used macramé rope to cover the base as it is a little softer and kinder on the fingers than jute or sisal rope. The base was cut from 18mm MDF, but can be made easily from sturdy cardboard. I would suggest using three layers of thick card glued together, just so it gives extra stiffness for when you are wrapping the rope around it; the boxes used to display fruit at the supermarket are perfect for this purpose, and the local shop manager is normally always happy to give them away. Gluing on the driftwood horizontally will brace the shape, and make it even stronger.

The little houses were cut from a single piece of plank that washed up on the beach, but if you can't find anything the right thickness, air dry clay makes a great substitute as you can make the buildings to the appropriate dimensions for your design. It is also available

to purchase from some of the suppliers in the directory. Everything else was foraged from the greenhouse, friendly carpenters and my home; one of the pieces of mesh for the tiny fishing nets is actually a small section of tulle, snipped from my wedding dress underskirt. Once you have completed the project, any leftover components can be glued to a flat piece of driftwood to make a seashore scene.

If you don't have easy access to the beach, a quick walk in the woods will often provide some interesting pieces you can use as an alternative to driftwood, and you can often find branches or sticks without bark. Allow to dry under cover outside for a few days (to allow any tiny creatures to escape). Clean with a wire brush to remove any moss and debris, then give a quick coat of white paint for a nautical feel; I find a mix of one part white emulsion to one part water works very well, as it looks clean and fresh but still allows a little of the natural pattern of the wood to show through. Failing that, pub skips are also a constant source of useful bits and pieces.

Lastly, a note of caution. Many of the nautically themed home decor items you see in shops feature shells or dried starfish. However, the Marine Conservation Society advises against purchasing these items for decorations as they are often unsustainably sourced on a factory scale, and are harming many ecosystems; far better to wander the beach and find some local treasures.

MATERIALS

- 45cm diameter wooden or cardboard base, with a width of roughly 10cm.
- 40m of 8mm macramé rope
- Long piece of driftwood for the base of the diorama (the piece shown is 58cm long, and 2cm wide at the top)
- Four or five little wooden houses, with a base that will fit on your piece of driftwood (the ones pictured are 2cm deep, and between 3 and 5cm wide).
- Cotton yarn
- Reel wire
- 30mm nails for chimneys and fencing
- 40mm nail for the flagpole
- Pistachio shells
- Wooden kebab skewers
- A chip fork (we had fish and chips after beachcombing, so I kept one of the unused ones. Wooden disposable coffee stirrers are also ideal.)
- Thick metal foil (I used a well-washed ready meal tin from some rather good thick cut chips)
- Two metal washers
- Fabric scraps or 9mm cotton ribbon
- 20cm length of dowel, for the lighthouse
- A scrap of fishing net (the white netting used to package fresh garlic in supermarkets makes an ideal alternative)
- A couple of pieces of lichen, scavenged from the woods (reindeer moss also works well and is available online)

- PVA glue
- Glue gun
- Hammer
- Wire cutters
- Flat-nosed pliers
- Sharp fabric scissors
- Sharpie (a fine-tipped permanent marker pen. I used black and grey)
- White chalk paint (ideal for this project as you can use it on both wood and metal)
- Acrylic paint
- Paintbrushes
- Fine grade sandpaper
- Sticky tape
- Needle and thread
- Needle-nose pliers

1. Take one end of your rope and hold at the back of the wooden base, then start to wrap the cord round, covering the loose tail as you go. Because you are wrapping a circle, and we want to keep the rope nice and flat to the base, you will inevitably end up with gaps, but that is fine, keep going!

2. Once you have gone all the way round, stick a little bit of Sellotape or masking tape around the rope at the point where you want to cut it, then snip with scissors; the tape ensures that the cord won't immediately start to fray.

3. Glue the end on the back of the form, then attach a new piece and start wrapping in the opposite direction, covering up any places where the wood is still showing through.

4. Wrap some tape around the rope at the point you have finished and cut through, to bind the ends. Fix the end of the rope in place at the back of the form, using a generous dab of hot glue to secure the end.

5. Take a 15cm length of the rope, fold into a U-shape and stitch securely to the back of the wreath to make the hanging loop.

6. Pour some of your chalk paint on to an old plate, and then add a good-sized blob of blue acrylic paint. Using a large brush, dip it into the paint (don't mix it up) and then apply to the driftwood in wide generous sweeps to create a seashore effect. Leave to dry.

7. To make the little houses, I painted the walls and roof with some leftover chalk paint I found under the sink (in this case, Rustoleum chalky white); it has a lovely flat texture, and I think the colours are reminiscent of a little windswept fishing village.

8. I added various colours of matt acrylic paint to the white paint to make all the cottages look slightly different.

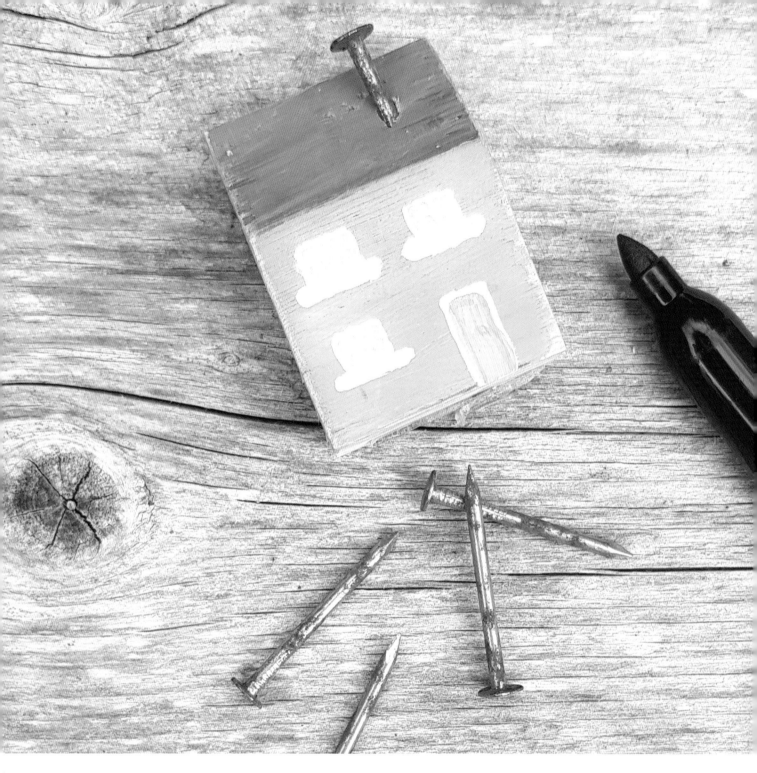

9. Once the walls and roof are dry, give the corners and edges a quick rub with the sandpaper to make them a little more weathered. Add some white squares for the window frames, then draw on the panes in either black paint or Sharpie.

10. Hammer a couple of small nails into each roof to make the chimneys.

11. Paint the dowel with a generous layer of white chalk paint, and

then add red stripes to make the lighthouse. Draw on a few windows using the Sharpie.

12. Paint the washers with two coats of chalk paint, and then add some detail in red to make the life rings. I glued one of the rings on to a 4cm piece of driftwood, just to add a little height.

13. To make the bunting, lay out a piece of wire across the top third of the ring in order to work out how long it will need to be; make sure you've got an extra 10cm at either end to give you enough to attach it.

14. Cut fifteen or so 5cm lengths of ribbon or fabric scraps and lay them out on your work surface, right-side down. Paint half of each one with a layer of PVA and lay the wire out across them, making sure it lies roughly in the middle.

15. Fold the ribbon over so the wire is at the fold, then press firmly and leave for a couple of hours to dry. Once the glue has dried the flags should be lovely and stiff; snip into flags or bunting with the sewing scissors.

16. Repeat this procedure with the 40mm nail, cutting a 6cm section of ribbon, applying glue and then folding it over the nail just below the head. Snip into a flag shape when dry.

17. The little rope ladder was made from a couple of wooden kebab skewers. Cut the skewer into six 2cm sections (you might find the secateurs easier than the scissors for this job, as the cut pieces do have a tendency to ping off all over the place). Snip two 20cm lengths of thin string or cotton yarn and tie to the skewer sections to make the ladder; the easiest way to do this is make a loop with the yarn then feed the end through the loop to make the knot. Insert the

skewer and then pull the yarn taut to tighten it. Add a couple of tiny blobs of PVA to the rungs of the ladder to secure.

18. Make the little boats by applying two coats of chalk paint to the pistachio shells. Cut a section of wooden coffee stirrer or chip fork and glue into each one with PVA, to make the benches.

19. Draw three rough outlines of seagulls on to the base of the metal tin, and then cut out with scissors. (If you are not feeling too artistic, a basic chunky 'V' shape will work very nicely). Apply two generous coats of white chalk paint and then add a little detail to the wing-tips in grey and black Sharpie.

20. Cut three 2cm pieces of reel wire, bend into a U-shape and glue to the back of the seagulls to make a hanging loop.

21. Cut three 15cm lengths of reel wire, and using the pliers, bend a little loop into each of the ends. Attach the seagulls and then close up with the pliers.

22. Work out where you want the little houses and the lighthouse to go, and make a small pencil mark. Remove the houses.

23. Hammer some little nails into the large driftwood base to make the fence.

24. Wrap a piece of reel wire around one of the nails, and then continue to loop it tightly round the rest. Give the end of the wire

a gentle squeeze with the pliers just to finish it in place. Dab on a couple of spots of chalk paint to highlight the wire.

25. Hammer the nail with the flag on it into one end of the driftwood.

26. Turn the wreath over and glue the bunting to the back, so that the flags hang down, then add the seagull wires at different heights. Bend their wings a little to give the illusion of flight.

27. Place the wreath right side up. Heat up your hot glue gun, and applying a good thick layer to the back of the driftwood, attach it to the wreath.

28. Glue the houses, ladder, fishing boats and lighthouse onto the front of the wreath.

29. Cut some tiny pieces of fishing net and glue on, bunching it up into little piles to cover any areas you wish to cover up. Add any lichen or reindeer moss to make small bushes.

30. Hang your wreath on the wall and sit back and dream of those heady summer days at the beach.

CHAPTER FIVE
LOVELY LAVENDER

LAVENDER IS TRADITIONALLY a staple of cottage gardens, and is a wonderful addition to any wreath. Often used in aromatherapy, the fragrance is said to promote calm and well-being, and is used as a treatment for insomnia, stress, anxiety and even mild pain, such as menstrual cramps and headaches.

The lavender plant, as we know it, dates back 2,500 years to India, the Middle East and the Mediterranean. Used for medicine, perfume and cooking in classical times, the plant was widely used throughout the Roman Empire. In fact the word 'lavender' comes from the Latin 'lavare', meaning 'to wash'; Roman soldiers used to travel with lavender-scented soap for its antibacterial properties, and Pliny the Elder extolled its virtues in easing a variety of medical disorders.

It does seem that every time you open a newspaper or magazine these days the emphasis is on sleep, whether it is how much we should be getting, or why we are not getting enough. Create one of these wonderful lavender wreaths using either fresh or dried flowers and hang above your bed, then inhale that fabulous scent to soothe you to dreamy oblivion. Fresh flowers will dry out in a couple of weeks, but the arrangement should last for years; refresh the scent with a couple of drops of essential oil every few weeks when necessary.

Both the lavender heart and the candle ring are both made using the same technique. The stems are cut to the same length and made into little bundles using florist's tape; the bundles are then spaced out and tied onto a base. Fresh lavender is quite pliable and forgiving so you can make smaller wreaths, candle garlands and even napkin rings; however, make sure that when you wire the

stems on to any base you pull the reel quite tightly, as they will shrink considerably as they dry out. The advantage of dried lavender is that it is available all year round, but it is slightly more liable to break at the stalk, so is not so well suited to the tiniest of projects.

Incidentally, once you have picked or purchased your lavender, don't put it in water. It has evolved in hot dry conditions and will survive very nicely for a few days in a cool place until you need it.

I had a lovely forty-eight hours where my fridge was filled with six huge bunches, and released a wonderfully calming scent whenever I opened the door; my vintage cheddar had a slightly floral note that I wasn't expecting, but the lavender was in top condition when I retrieved it.

LARGE LAVENDER SUMMER HEART

The lavender heart featured is a quite a sizeable arrangement and measures about 50cm x 50cm when completed. It requires a good quantity of lavender, so if you are making a smaller one you will obviously require less; 150 stems should cover a 25cm heart very nicely. Whilst working on this project, I wired the bundles not just to the top but also to the inside and the outside of the form as I worked round it. This resulted in a much fuller-looking shape.

MATERIALS

- Lavender, roughly 800 stems, or four bunches if purchased from a lavender farm.
- Pliable twigs (honeysuckle works well)
- 30cm of 30mm wide ribbon, if you would like to finish it with a bow
- Scissors
- Floristry reel wire
- Floristry tape
- 50cm garden wire (I used a mild steel wire as it is quite easy to bend)
- Wire cutters
- Flat-nosed pliers

1. First of all, make your base. Taking one end of the garden wire, form a ring that is roughly 40cm in diameter, then weave the ends in and out to strengthen the circle. Use a little tape to cover over the ends of the wire to ensure you don't catch yourself on the ends.

2. Bend the circle into a heart shape, ensuring the taped ends are on one long side of the heart; this will make it easier to shape. Using flat-nosed pliers, make a point at the bottom of the circle, and then pulling the opposing side of the ring towards it, pinch again to give a defined shape.

3. I always think it is a good idea to add the hanging loop at this stage, rather than wait until the end of the project and wonder how you are going to hang it. Cut a 20cm length of wire, and fold in half. Twist the ends together and then wrap these around the top indent of the heart a couple of times, pinching it together with flat-nosed pliers so it is secure.

4. Take your foraged twigs and attach them around the heart to form a sturdy base. Start at the bottom of the heart, and, holding them tightly against the wire form, wrap round with the reel wire, adding in more twigs when necessary.

5. Organise your lavender into bundles. Take twenty stems of lavender and, using the floristry tape, tie them into a little bunch, ensuring all the heads are roughly together. Trim the stems with the secateurs so the bunch is about 15cm long. Repeat, until you have forty-one bundles.

6. Split the bundles in to two piles of twenty (setting the last one aside for later), and roughly lay them round your heart form, to give you an idea of how closely you will need to space them.

7. Tie the reel wire on to the form, at the bottom point of the heart.

8. Take one of the bundles, lay it on top of the left-hand side of the heart, pointing downwards, so the blooms are just covering the bottom of the heart. Wire in place, starting just underneath the flower heads, giving it a few wraps around the stems to secure it in place.

9. Add more bunches and continue to wire them around the ring until you reach the centre of the heart, ensuring that the flower heads cover up the stalks on the previous bundle.

10. Begin wiring the right-hand side of the form, again making sure the bundles are pointing downwards.

11. When you reach the 'V' at the top of the heart, tie off the wire, and cut the stalks from the last bundle off, flush with the metal form.

12. When both sides are covered to your satisfaction (you might want to tuck the odd sprig in here and there to fatten it up a bit), take the last bundle and wire in place with the buds pointing upwards to cover the 'V' shape

section of the heart. The lavender will contract as it dries so make sure you pull the wire nice and tight. Snip off the stalks to leave neat ends.

13. Tie the ribbon over the base of the hanging loop, letting the tails drape down to cover any joins.

14. You may find for the first couple of days your wreath will shed some of the buds, but that will soon stop as the loose ones all drop. If they continue to drop, I find a quick blast with some fragrance-free hair spray does the trick instantly.

LAVENDER CANDLE WREATH

Candle rings are very popular in Scandinavia, and are a great way to use up leftover stems. Perfect for a garden party, this pretty circle not only looks wonderful but will release a gorgeous summery scent for your guests. Made in the same way as the large heart wreath, it is created by tying smaller bundles on to a wire form. (Please don't leave the candle unattended or let it burn too close to the flowers).

MATERIALS

- Lavender (about 200 heads)
- Garden wire
- Wire cutters
- Floristry tape
- Secateurs
- Large pillar candle measuring 8cm x 20cm

1. Cut a 30cm length of wire and bend into a circle with a diameter 14cm across (this will ensure you will be able to fit it over the candle without damaging the lavender).

2. Tape the ends of the wire securely.

3. Prepare your lavender bundles. Gather twenty stems and lay them out so the heads are all vaguely together, then tape them into a bunch using the floristry tape.

4. Snip the stems off with the secateurs so the bundle measures approximately 15cm in length.

5. Tie your reel wire on to the wire circle, and then start to add the lavender bunches, wiring around the stems as you go.

KITCHEN HERB HEART

This aromatic heart will look glorious hanging from a kitchen dresser, and is an attractive way to dry and display herbs. I believe it is currently very fashionable to add a scatter of lavender buds to one's shortbread to add a floral flavour (although why you'd want to ruin a perfectly good biscuit and make it taste of shampoo is

beyond me). Sage and rosemary are also particularly well suited to drying in this way. Pick them on a warm evening in late summer when the herbs are at their fragrant height and hang in your kitchen somewhere dry and airy. Keep them out of direct sunlight (and away from steamy saucepans), then simply pluck a few leaves next time you are knocking up a stuffing or some Pommes Parmentier.

MATERIALS

- 25cm willow heart
- 40cm hanging ribbon
- Reel wire
- Lavender
- Sage
- Rosemary

1. Tie the hanging ribbon to the top of the heart, adding a blob of hot glue if necessary to make sure it is nicely central and does not slip off to one side.

2. Tie the reel wire to the point at the base of the heart. Picking up one sprig at a time and pointing it downwards, attach the leaves by holding them against the form and then wrapping with the reel wire, pulling it as tight as possible.

3. Lay the next sprig on the wreath so it overlaps the wire and join and repeat until you reach the hanging ribbon.

4. Snip off the reel wire and tie off securely.

5. Begin the process again at the bottom, this time coming up the other side, bending the sprigs around the curves as you go.

6. Hang it up and start cooking.

LAVENDER BOTTLE

If you have a few green stems left over, why not try making a lavender bottle? Popular as a country craft in France, they make a sweet little gift and are perfect for scenting drawers or airing cupboards. Ensure you pull the ribbon quite tight as you are weaving, as the lavender stalks will shrink a little as they dry.

MATERIALS

- 5mm satin ribbon. 1.5m should be plenty

• Between thirteen and seventeen stems of lavender, 30cm long (make sure you have an odd number)
• Scissors
• Needle and thread or a dab of hot glue
• A spoon

1. Strip the lavender stalks of any leaves, and make sure you are using the longest ones you have available.

2. Lay the lavender out so the heads are bunched up neatly, then take one end of the ribbon and tie them all together.

3. Take the spoon and use it push down hard on the top of the stems; this means they will be easier to bend at the next stage.

4. Fold all the stems down so you are in effect creating a little cage for all the flower heads, thus making the bottle shape.

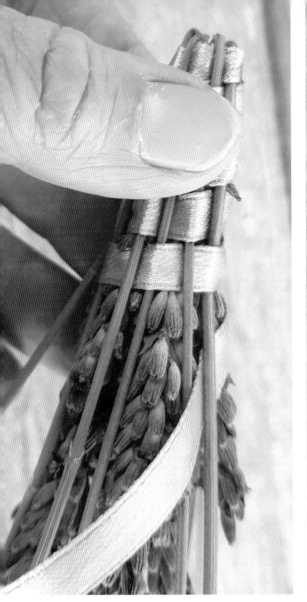 

5. Start to weave the ribbon in and out of the stalks.

6. Pull the ribbon tightly after each round, and ensure it fits snugly against the row above; continue until you have reached a natural end point, then snip off the ribbon and secure with either a couple of stitches or a blob of glue.

7. Trim off the stems neatly, then using the leftover ribbon, tie a bow over the join to hide it. The scent should last quite a long time but is easily refreshed by rolling the bottle between your hands, or by adding a couple of drops of essential oil.

CHAPTER SIX

SUMMER CELEBRATION

WHETHER IT IS for a special celebration such as a wedding, or a garden party to mark a family event, a confection of summer blooms will always add a beautiful touch to your table or garden (even as you sit there huddled in your cagoule, waiting for the rain shower to pass). If it is very warm outside, I would advise keeping the wreath in the shade until it is needed, to avoid the flowers wilting prematurely; hang on a north-facing door or display on a dresser inside until your party starts.

In earlier times, making a floral arrangement was simple; one simply took oasis foam, soaked it until it was thoroughly soggy and then poked some flowers into it. Nowadays we are all much more conscious of the environmental impact of our hobbies, so oasis is no longer a favoured material. Not only does it not biodegrade, but as any residual water is tipped away microplastics are carried into the hydrological cycle. As a result I think it is much better to use moss for these floral projects; not only does it have a lovely organic feel to work with, but it can be rehydrated and used again many times before being composted. The wire base can also be repurposed and with care should last for years.

To keep your flowers in tip-top condition it is important that you treat them like little pets who are constantly thirsty. Cut stems have a tendency to heal over, so if you are buying them from a florist or supermarket snip the tip off the stem at an angle as soon as possible, to ensure maximum uptake of water. Do this every couple of days (even when they are in an arrangement), and they will last much longer. Don't leave them in full sun, and make sure all your tools, secateurs and vases are scrupulously clean to avoid any chance of infection. In addition, moss can not only hold up to twenty times its own weight in water, but also has antiseptic properties. Sphagnum moss was traditionally used as a wound dressing in the First World War as it has a low pH and inhibits bacterial growth, so is the ideal medium for keeping your fresh components as healthy as possible.

As to the composition of your design, I think it is most effective (and economical) to use a few large statement blooms, with the spaces filled by a mixture of smaller flowers and foliage. In this arrangement, dusky lisianthus flowers provide the colour, while white clouds of gypsophila add a soft romantic feel. Wired sprays of wheat give a contemporary touch and a little height to the arrangement. The flowers and foliage can be added to the moss wreath in two ways. In the first method one can attach jute string to the wire frame, bundle the fresh material into sprigs and simply wrap them on (as in the Kitchen Herb Heart). However, here I wanted a little more height, rather than having everything laid flat against the form, so the sprigs were inserted individually until the wreath was covered. The benefit of doing it in this way is that you can continue to adjust your design until you are happy with it, rather than having to unwrap everything.

SUMMER CELEBRATION

MATERIALS

- 30cm wire ring
- Fresh floristry moss
- Eucalyptus
- Lisianthus
- Gypsophila
- American oak leaves (these were lightly sprayed with a touch of pink water-based paint) or other large leaves
- Wheat
- Reel wire
- Jute string
- Bundle of 30cm raffia strands, for hanging

1. Make your form. Ensuring your moss is good and damp, tie the jute string on to the outside of the wire frame, then gather a good handful and squidge it on to the frame. Wrap the string over the top, through the hole and back round, pulling on the cord tightly to secure.

2. Keep adding handfuls of moss and wrapping with the string, so that the wraps are about 4cm apart. Tie off when you arrive back at the beginning.

3. Tie a raffia hanging loop at the top of the wreath.

4. Snip the ends off the eucalyptus stems at an angle and push into the moss, both around the outside and the inside of the frame.

5. Add the other pieces of large foliage, once again snipping the ends off first.

6. Bundle three or four wheat heads into a sprig and wire together, leaving the wire attached. Snip the stems off so the bundle is roughly 15cm long, and then

wire on to the frame. Repeat until you have five or six bunches of wheat spread evenly around the circle.

7. Cut the stems off the lisianthus and push them into the moss around the central spine of the wreath.

8. Lastly, add the gypsophila to fill in any gaps, tucking them in behind the wheat bundles to help them stay propped up.

9. Spray with water every couple of days to keep the moss damp, or, even better, leave it out in a rain shower to refresh it.

CHAPTER SEVEN

UPCYCLED HESSIAN

FABRIC WREATHS MAKE a great alternative to wooden or straw ones, as you can tailor the colour of the material to the decor of your home. I particularly like using hessian as it adds a pleasing rustic feel to any creation, and is particularly well suited to festive themes. If you have an artisan coffee roaster nearby, they may well have coffee sacks available for sale for a couple of pounds, and these often have very attractive printed designs (they are also available on eBay). You can also use cotton fabric or old sheets; you could cut the basic strips with pinking shears to create an interesting texture to the edge of wreath, or turn the fabric tube inside out before you proceed to form the wreath into a circle if you prefer a neater finish.

Both the wreaths featured here start out with the same base, made from recycled pipe lagging and an old wire coat-hanger. I strongly recommend making friends with an amenable plumber or builder before you start this project, as most bathroom remodelling projects will result in leftover lagging. Old swimming pool noodles also work well; just increase the width of the fabric strips and omit the wire.

REUSABLE HESSIAN WREATH

The joy of this wreath is that you can slide your decorative elements into the metal rings, and then just replace them whenever you fancy making some changes; it's a great way to add a little fresh greenery to your home depending on what is available in the garden. Even just a few sprigs of evergreen will look wonderful in the depths of winter, but I particularly like to use ivy when there are no flowers in bloom. Cut 15cm long lengths of foliage and tuck them down

through the first loop and out through the second, freeing up any leaves that get caught. Push your next piece of foliage down through the next D-ring and so on, adding the odd flower for colour. To begin with, the stems will fit quite loosely into the rings, but as you begin to work more greenery into the form they should all hold together nicely. Four or five sewn down one side will give a more contemporary feel; if you want them to go all the way round, use more flexible leaves so you can bend them round. These bases also work very well for non-foliage decoration; think lollipops for a children's party and candy canes for Christmas.

MATERIALS

(this will make a wreath approx 50cm in diameter)

- 90cm of hessian, 90cm wide
- 100cm of pipe lagging
- 110cm of mild steel gardening wire. A wire coat-hanger makes an excellent alternative, as it measures roughly 111cm.
- Needle and strong thread
- Hot glue gun and glue
- Pliers
- Duct or wide masking tape
- 20mm metal D-rings (five if you wish the ornamentation to be on just one side, and eleven if you would like it go all the way around).

1. Cut three strips from the hessian fabric, each one 30cm wide and 90cm long (the width of the fabric roll).

2. Thread your needle with a long double length of cotton and knot at the end.

3. Fold one of the strips of hessian in half lengthways, and using a long running stitch, sew up the open sides, making a tube into which you will slide the lagging. Try and make

it quite a tight fit, so the fabric won't sag as soon as you add any embellishments.

4. Leave a hem of at least 5cm, as this will leave enough space for the hessian to fray attractively, but not so much that it reaches the seam.

5. Thread the sewn section over the pipe lagging and draw up the cotton thread so the ruched hessian covers roughly one third of the tube, then stitch the thread in place to secure the gathers.

6. Repeat with the other two pieces of hessian, feeding in the pipe lagging, and then drawing up the thread and stitching in place.

7. Cut a 110cm length of wire, or unwrap your coat-hanger and straighten it out with the flat-nosed pliers.

8. Insert the wire into the pipe lagging and hessian tube, keeping all the seams to the left.

9. Cut a 10cm piece of duct tape. Poke one of the ends of the wire coat-hanger down the opposite end of the pipe lagging tube, then do the same with the other end, forming a circle.

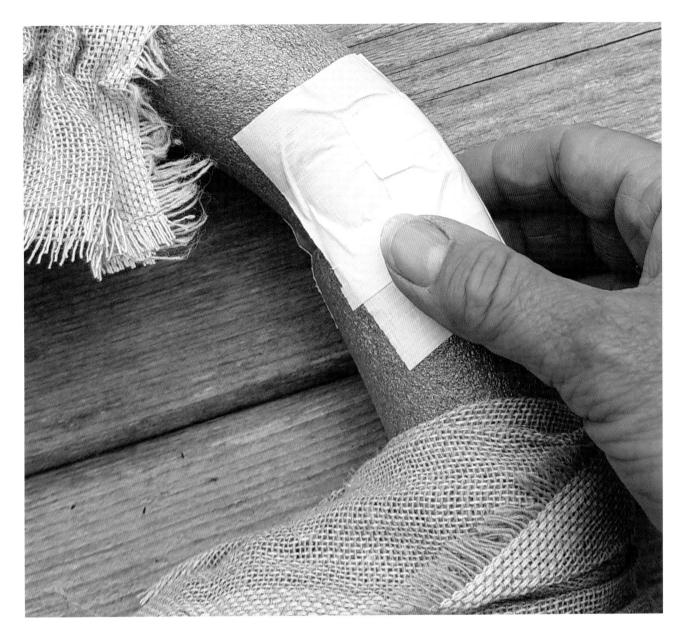

10. Holding the two ends firmly in place against each other, wrap them with the strip of duct tape to secure the pipe lagging into a round form.

11. Spread the gathered hessian evenly around the form, so the seam is outwards and the excess fabric forms a fringe.

12. Working quickly, run a line of glue over one edge of the hessian tube closest to you. Pull the edge of the next section over the glue and press down to secure (do be careful, as the glue will be hot and can squirt out unexpectedly through holes in the hessian).

13. Repeat at every join. Your circle should now be complete on one side, without any gaps showing through.

14. Turn the hessian form over and continue to glue the edges down in the same manner.

15. At this stage your hessian may well be fraying quite uncontrollably, but don't worry too much if it looks like a scarecrow's wedding hat, as it can be trimmed at the end.

16. Stitch one of the D-rings to the back of the wreath at the top to make your hanging loop.

17. Working with doubled thread, stitch the other D-rings on to the wreath about 5cm apart, with the flat side down.

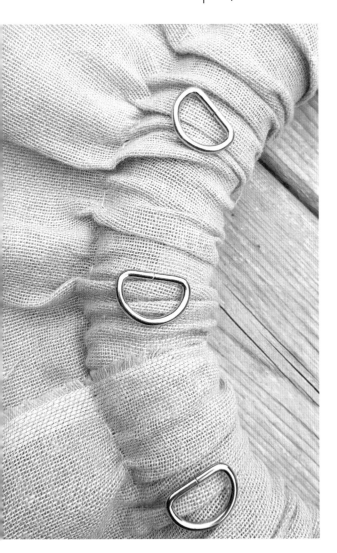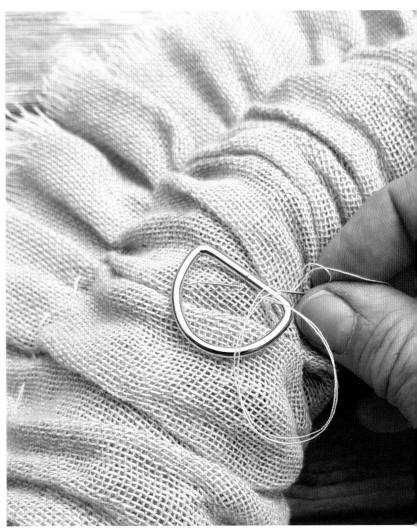

18. Pull out any trailing hessian threads to give a fringed finish, and snip off any that refuse to play nicely.

HARVEST FESTIVAL

I was originally going to call this 'Blackberry and Apple Crumble' as that was what I had for pudding the night before, but then I found some beautifully fat rosehips out on a walk by the river and decided they were destined for this project. I would definitely suggest wearing gloves when you start to weave in the hawthorn and blackberries as the possibilities for getting scratched are numerous.

MATERIALS

- One x 50cm hessian wreath
- Ivy, with flowers
- Hawthorn sprigs and berries
- Rosehips
- 6–8 small apples
- 15–20 heads of wheat
- Blackberries
- Gardening gloves
- Coat-hanger
- Reel wire

1. Begin by winding your ivy sprigs in and out of the D-rings as this will add a little structure and is a good (unprickly) base on which to work.

2. Tuck the hawthorn in next, spreading the leaves out to cover the metal fixings.

3. Cut the wheat to a length of 10cm and wire two or three stems together. Repeat to make five or six bundles and wire them into the hawthorn so that they stick up at an angle.

4. Tuck the blackberries into the D-rings, adding a twist of wire to hold them in place if necessary.

5. To attach the apples, unwind the coat-hanger and push it through the base of the fruit to make a hole. Aim off to one side as it's much

harder to try and push it through the core. Insert a 20cm length of reel wire through the hole, twist together and wire into the base.

6. Push the rosehips firmly into the foliage, tucking the stems into the wire behind the apples.

GRANNY'S MAKE DO AND MEND

This lovely neutral wreath has a definite vintage edge to it, which would be wonderful for a home-style wedding, and is made in exactly the same way as the project above, up to the addition of the D-rings. Everything used for this project was either recycled, or came from my Granny's sewing box and her legendary 'Box of Useful Fabric, Button and Bits and Pieces', and I think it is a great way to showcase old family items. However, you could use gingham ribbon, padded hearts and buttons for a cosy New England feel, or Scandi-themed fat squares or felt gingerbread men for a Nordic

look. Shades of blue with rope wrapping would look great in a nautically themed bathroom.

MATERIALS

- One x 50cm hessian wreath
- Fabric strips 90cm long by 7cm wide, for the roses (I used a mixture of hessian and vintage Laura Ashley fabric)
- Scraps of ribbon and lace (in this case an old lace curtain and some vintage fabric trim)
- Vintage buttons, knitting needles, thimbles and cotton reels

1. Cut an edge from the lace curtain and glue or stitch it on to the ring, along with any other pretty trimmings you have, wrapping them round the curve of the ring and finishing them off at the back. I

also found an old tape measure so I added a couple of extra lengths of that too; leave the ends sticking out as you can trim them later.

2. To make the roses, cut a 5cm x 5cm square of hessian and set aside. Heat up your glue gun.

3. Prepare a strip of material 90cm by 7cm. With the length of fabric off to the left, fold down the right-hand corner towards you, at a sloping angle.

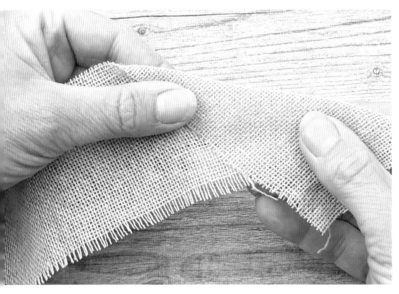

4. Take the far right end of the corner and begin to roll fabric towards you, along the folded edge. As soon as you start to run out of a folded section to roll, take the material in your left hand and turn it away from you, making a new folded section.

5. Continue to roll and fold, until you have used all the fabric.

6. Once you have an attractive fat rose, take your glue gun and squirt some adhesive over the 5cm hessian square (I would suggest using an upside-down tea plate as a work surface as this will stop you accidentally sticking the rose to your dining room table).

7. Press the rose down on to the hot glue, and then squeeze some more down in between the petal folds to secure them.

8. Allow the glue to cool, then trim off the excess hessian round the base.

9. Repeat with either fabric or some of the excess hessian to make five roses in total.

10. The little rosettes are made with strips of ribbon, cut to a length of 14cm from a 9mm ribbon. (Cutting the ends of the ribbon at an angle rather than straight across will help to stop it fraying.) Thread your needle with a double thread and then sew all the way along with a running stitch along one edge.

11. Draw the thread up and secure with a couple of stitches to form the rosette, then sew on a button in the centre of the circle to finish it off.

12. Poke the knitting needles through the hessian, adding a blob of glue to secure if necessary.

13. Stitch or glue the large roses on to the form, then add the little ribbon rosettes.

14. Stitch or glue on any other little embellishments you would like to add. I found a little card with buttons on

and a couple of thimbles, so I tucked those in between the roses, then attached some old sewing thread reels for a little colour.

15. Lastly, add the buttons. I strongly believe that you can't have too many buttons on any project, so attach them in copious quantities.

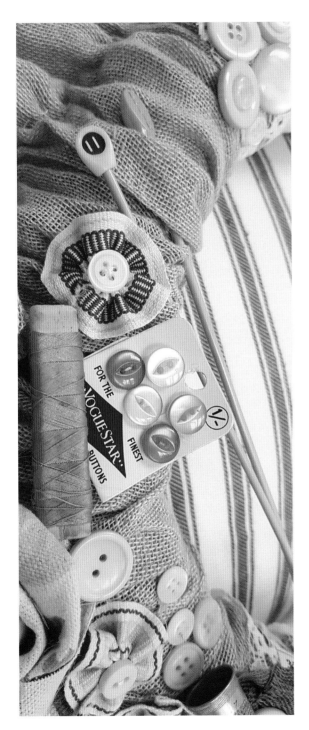

CHAPTER EIGHT

POM-POM
WREATH

THIS GORGEOUS WREATH is so gloriously tactile that I have yet to see anyone walk past it without giving one of the pom-poms a little squidge, and it is a great way to use up wool left over from other projects. It would look pretty in shades of pastel as a nursery gift, and the addition of a few tiny glass baubles will instantly give it a festive feel for a Christmas-time front door. I have seen them

in shops at Christmas at pretty extortionate prices, but they are so quick and easy to knock up over a couple of evenings, why not make your own?

MATERIALS

- One straw wreath form, 20cm in diameter
- Double knitting wool in assorted colours, equivalent to 1,000m (the length of yarn in a ball is usually written on the packaging)
- Glue gun and sticks
- Acrylic paint, to match your main shade
- Tiny glass baubles (optional)

1. Make your pom-poms using the method outlined below. You will need roughly twenty-two pom-poms made using your hand, and six made with a fork.

2. Paint the straw wreath with a coat of acrylic paint, just so that if there are any gaps between the pom-poms the base will not show through too obviously. Allow to dry.

3. Glue the pom-poms on to the base; start by gluing thirteen of the larger ones on to the outside by applying a generous blob of glue on to the straw and then pushing the pom-pom firmly on to it until the adhesive has set. Once all thirteen are attached, turn the form over and just add a few more squirts of glue along the join to secure them properly.

4. Repeat the procedure to attach six small pom-poms to the inside of the form, once again turning it over and adding a little extra glue.

5. Fill in the gaps with the last nine pom-poms.

6. Arrange your little glass baubles so they nestle in between the wool balls, and attach using the glue gun so any metal fixings are tucked away out of sight.

Here are two fabulously easy ways of making pom-poms that don't use any special equipment, apart from a fork. So much easier than using cardboard circles (and having to push the yarn through an ultimately tiny hole), both these methods can be adjusted to increase or decrease the dimensions of the final ball. The number of wraps necessary will depend on the thickness of your wool; for the method listed below, a double-knitting yarn was used. A chunky wool will require less winding, whereas a thinner, silkier thread will require more. If you wish to make pom-poms to hang on your Christmas tree or from a garland, take the two ends of yarn you used to wrap them in a bundle and knot them together to make a hanging loop, before trimming the pom-poms into shape.

To increase the density of your pom-pom, simply wrap the wool round a few more times (I would suggest in multiples of ten), and to decrease the diameter, simply use fewer fingers. Four fingers, two hundred wraps and a DK wool gives a pom-pom roughly 8cm in diameter when trimmed, and a fork should give you a ball of around 6cm.

1. To make a small pom-pom using a fork, cut a 20cm length of yarn and drape through the centre at the base of the tines, back to front to back. Tuck it out of the way in your hand while you make the pom-pom.

2. Take your ball of wool and hold one end against the tines. Now just continue wrapping the wool round and around 150 times,

ensuring that you have left a gap at the base of the tines. Try and keep the wrapping together at this stage; if the bundle spreads out too far it will make it more difficult to tie it tightly.

3. Draw the 20cm separate piece of yarn up between the middle prongs at the top, through the hole at the bottom. Tie the two ends together as tightly as possible.

4. Slide the bundle off the fork.

5. Using sharp scissors, snip all the loops you have made in order to create the basic pom-pom shape.

6. At this stage you will probably think, 'oh, that looks disastrous', but fear not; start to trim the pom-pom little by little into a ball, and it will look much more presentable. I would suggest

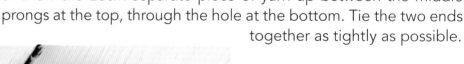

doing the trimming over a tray or straight into the waste paper basket as the mess you can make at this stage is considerable.

To make a large pom-pom, the method is pretty much the same, you just use your hand instead of a fork.

1. Cut a 20cm length of yarn and drape over your second and third fingers, then leave it there, tucking it out of the way in your hand.

2. Wrap the wool round 150 times, leaving it loose enough that you can still move your fingers. If you would like to make a ball with two colours, just wrap the yarn from two balls at once; the benefit of this method is that you will only need to make seventy-five wraps.

3. Now take your initial length of yarn and draw it up around the yarn bundle you have made. Loop one end under the other, and draw up, then slide the bundle off your hand in order to finish the knot.

4. Snip through the loops with sharp scissors to make the rough pom-pom.

5. Trim the ends to tidy up the spherical shape.

POM-POM GARLAND

If you have excess pom-poms (or are just in the pom-pom making zone), a quick and easy garland will continue the theme throughout your decor. The addition of two lovely fluffy tassels at either end enables you to hang it up without having to hide any unsightly ends.

MATERIALS

- Pom-poms (leave the long tails on while you are trimming them)
- Yarn
- Stiff card

1. Make the cord for your garland. Take 120cm of three different colours of yarn, knot together and plait them until you reach a metre

in length (I find the easiest way to do this is by safety pinning the whole thing to a cushion while I am plaiting. Double knot the ends, then knot again; you want this to be as large as possible to stop it slipping out from the tassel.

2. To make a tassel, cut a piece of card measuring 15cm x 20cm.

3. Wind your yarn around the length of the card, starting with the free end at the bottom.

4. After fifty wraps, snip through all the wool at one end, and lay the bundle out flat on your work surface.

5. Taking a 20cm piece of wool, lay it underneath your pile of threads at right angles, half way down the bundle.

6. Lie the knot on your plaited cord over the top of the bundle, ensuring it is further down than the midway point. Snuggle it down into the wool, then tie the short piece of yarn into a double knot as tightly as possible.

7. Pick up the plaited cord, and let all the tassel ends fall down, brushing them out if necessary.

8. Place another 20cm length of yarn under the tassel so a 5cm tail is poking out towards the left. Draw up and tie tightly.

9. Wrap the long tail round the tassel to make the 'waist', then tie off the end using the short tail.

10. Snip off the excess wool and then snuggle the knot down in between the wrapped yarn so it is hidden.

11. Make a second tassel, repeating the process with the other end of the plaited cord.

12. Tie your pom-poms on to the cord using their long tails, sliding them around to they are spread out evenly. Snip off the tails so they are the same length as the pom-pom strands.

CHAPTER NINE

COSY CROCHET

COSY NEUTRALS ARE perfect for adding a touch of Nordic hygge to your winter home, and these Scandi-style wreaths are so quick to make that you can easily knock one or two up in an evening. Made with extra chunky wool, you don't even need a crochet hook, just your fingers. With many of these chunky yarns, they tend to get fluffy quite quickly, so it is worth trying to touch your work as little as possible while you are crocheting. I have found that a quick squirt of hairspray dusted across the wreath when you have finished will help stop it getting fuzzy over time. Do not, whatever you do, attempt to eat buttered toast while you are working with cream wool (as I did), as the result will look like a grubby toddler has been let loose with a sheep.

Rather than having your work facing you as one would naturally do with traditional crochet, I find it easier to hold the wreath frame between my knees. While the wire frames are cheap and easily purchased, you might find that some of the soldering on the joints leaves a little to be desired and that there may be sharp ends poking out. In this case, I would suggest putting a small amount of masking tape over the problem, just to stop it snagging on your beautiful wool.

The cream wreath in the picture is made with an XL chunky knitting yarn, and is easily customised to change with the seasons; hang with a neutral ribbon for a Nordic look, then change to a forest green or ruby red for your front door at Christmas. The addition of some tiny bottle brush trees and tiny pom-poms completes the festive look.

COSY CROCHET WINTER WREATH

MATERIALS

- 30cm wire wreath frame
- 17m ball of XL chunky yarn
- Scissors
- Hot glue gun
- Twenty x 7mm white pom-poms
- Five small green bottle brush Christmas trees
- White chalk paint

- Old toothbrush
- White PVA glue
- Tweezers
- 1.5m of 5cm ribbon

1. A quick word of advice at this stage; keep the ball of wool to your left at all times. You will be passing loops of wool through the centre of the ring but the ball itself should never have to move.

2. Make a slip knot in the end of your yarn. Hold the wool in your left hand, and wrap it around the back of your right hand and up again so the yarn is crossed. Pass the wool around the back once more, draw through the loop at the back and pull, slipping the knot off your hand as you do so.

3. Hold the frame between your knees. Insert the index finger of your right hand through the slip knot, and hold it against the top of the frame, with the yarn going off towards the left.

4. Pass the wool down to the left, through the wreath and back up again, so it comes up between the frame and your finger.

5. Wrap the wool around the outside of your finger.

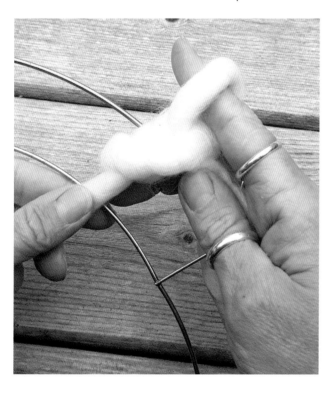
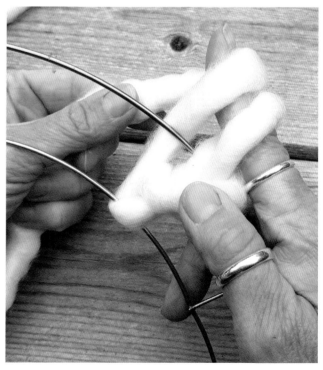

6. Pass the wool down and back through the centre of the ring, so the yarn is back on the left.

7. Take the wool back up so it is once again between your finger and the frame, and wrap it over the top of your finger, this time on the inside (there should now be three loops on your finger).

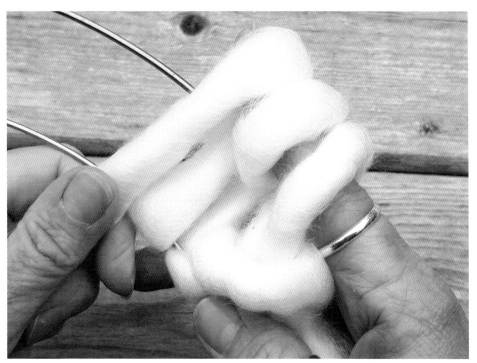

8. Holding the yarn tight, and still off to the left, take the loop closest to the tip of your finger and pull it through the two other loops. You should now have one loop on your finger again, thus completing the first stitch.

9. Repeat this manoeuvre all the way round until the wreath is covered; you will find your finger naturally angles towards first the right then the left as you complete both parts of the stitch.

10. Adjust the stitches so they are spread out evenly, and twisting the outer edge inwards so the lovely braided border is visible.

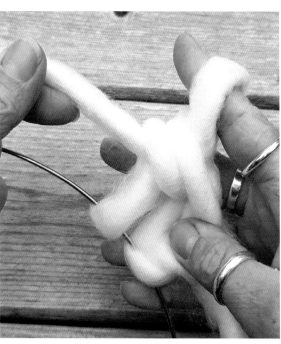

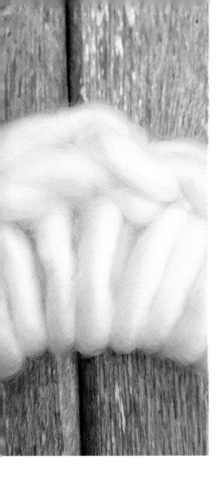

11. Snip the yarn so you have a 20cm tail and push it through your original slip knot from underneath. Pull it towards you, then tuck from front to back through the bottom of the next stitch along to the right. Fix at the rear with a blob of hot glue, snipping off any excess wool. This will now be the top of your wreath as the join will be covered by ribbon.

12. Trim off any fluff with scissors.

13. Mix a tablespoonful of white chalk paint with an equivalent amount of water. Dip the toothbrush in the paint and then push it down between the bristles of the trees, turning them as you go until they are completely covered with a snowy effect. Allow to dry.

14. Attach the little bottle brush trees at the bottom of the wreath with hot glue, nestling the trunks between the stitches. You might find the trees are wider than your wreath so they don't lie flat; in this case, trim the back with scissors before you apply the glue.

15. Glue the tiny pom-poms scattered over the wreath using PVA glue (I find it is easier to control than the hot glue gun when working on very tiny pieces). Pour the glue on to a saucer and then dip the pom-poms using tweezers, before scattering over the form. I used white ones here so they look liked falling snow, but a mixture of red and green would also look lovely.

16. Cut the ribbon into two 75cm pieces.

17. Loop through the top of the wreath and secure with a knot.

18. Tie the second piece of ribbon in a bow at the base of hanging loop, trimming the ends at an angle so they don't fray.

NORDIC NEUTRAL BRAIDED WREATH

The art of arm knitting to make huge chunky blankets is popular at the moment, where one uses one's hands and wrists instead of needles. While the concept appeals, the thought of being trapped in a vast wool web of my own creation, yet being unable to hop up and put the kettle on is frankly horrifying. The solution is this fabulously easy braiding trick. Not only can you make a wreath in just a few minutes, the braid can be stitched together in a spiral to create wonderfully textured cushions or wall hangings.

You can also thankfully put it down whenever you want. If you would like to make larger braided projects in this fashion I would suggest using two balls of wool at the same time, rather than cutting the yarn into equal lengths. Arm knitting wool is quite expensive compared to other yarns, but as you can make three or four wreaths from one ball it is a great way of batch making Christmas gifts.

MATERIALS

- Two x 600cm lengths of extra chunky arm-knitting yarn
- 30cm wire frame
- Scissors
- Hot glue gun
- Needle and thread
- 1.5m of 5cm ribbon

1. Tie a knot at the ends of the two pieces of yarn and lay the lengths out towards the left.

2. Bring the wool in a loop round to the right and back over, just above the knot.

3. Put your hand through the loop you have made, grasp the wool and pull it back through, making a loop the same size as your first one.

4. Keep your hand in the loop, pick up the wool and draw it through again, making yet another loop.

5. Continue until your braid is long enough to go all the way around your wreath. I would say at this point that it is worth having a trial go, just so you can get the hang of making all your loops the same size. In addition, keep the working yarn flat and side by side on the work surface so that your pattern will be even and not twisted.

6. Lay your braid out flat and, gently pulling on the knots, ensure that the stitches are even (it is quite forgiving at this stage so you can be experimental with it).

7. Put the starting knot through your last loop from front to back, to finish off. Secure in place with a blob of hot glue or a quick stitch.

8. Turn the braid upside down and place your wire frame on top.

9. Add generous blobs of glue all the way round to attach the braid to the form and press down firmly until dry.

10. Thread your needle with a double length of cotton and stitch around the frame to ensure the braid is fully secure (otherwise the wool will naturally start to droop).

11. Once the glue has dried, take a 75cm section of ribbon, pass it through the wreath and knot at the top to make the hanging loop.

12. Tie the other piece of ribbon in a lovely fat bow at the base of the hanging loop, trimming the ends at an angle so they don't fray.

CHAPTER TEN

WINTER WONDERLAND

NOTHING BRINGS TO mind the feel of a cosy winter's evening than a warm drink and a bowl full of pine cones (by which I mean the latter as decor, rather than pudding); this beautiful wintery wreath is so easy to make and you can even get the kids involved by going on a long walk together to forage for them. I like to have my pine cone extravaganza hanging up for most of the winter, so even if we sadly aren't snowed in, I can have a glass of hot rum, put on my pyjamas and a thick pair of ski socks and pretend I am in a snowy Alpine lodge.

Most people will naturally start looking for pine cones as soon as Christmas starts approaching, but this is one of those times when it is good to think ahead. The best time to collect them is actually in late summer or early autumn, after a particularly blustery night when a fresh crop has blown down. The squirrels will not yet have had a chance to get to them, and they won't have been trampled by other walkers.

Pine cones will close up when it is damp and cold, in order to protect their seeds. I tend to leave them outside under cover for a couple of days to allow any tiny creatures to escape, then wash them in the garden and bring them into the warm overnight so they are fully opened and dry. Many websites will advocate soaking the cones in bleach overnight to sterilise and clean them, but as they are porous they tend to absorb that 'I've just cleaned the kitchen' smell. If your cones are a little grubby, you can instead soak them in a sink of warm soapy water for twenty minutes, rinse well, and leave to dry. Alternatively half a cup of white vinegar stirred into a bucketful of water will also work effectively.

In my quest to make my designs as eco-lovely as possible, I was searching for an alternative to the kind of snow sprinkles you see in craft shops, the majority of which seem to be made of plastic.

The tips of the cones here still are dusted with a frosty snow effect, but the surprise ingredient is Maldon salt. Its lovely fat flakes add a pleasing frosty crunch to the whole project. Just be aware that if the wreath gets damp, the salt will dissolve, so keep your project indoors.

The wonderful thing about this wreath is that you can either leave it plain, for a minimalist log-cabin look, or tuck in tiny pieces of evergreen and the odd berry sprig; cypress and cedar are the perfect foliage for this as they will stay green for a couple of weeks. It also looks wonderful as a centrepiece for your Christmas table when laid down flat. Add a large Kilner jar in the middle and fill with battery-operated fairy lights or a large pillar candle for a little festive sparkle. Leftover pine cones can be glued together to make small candle rings, or glued on wooden napkin rings to coordinate with your table. Alternatively, the wreath looks fabulous sprayed black, with the addition of a couple of pipe cleaner spiders and some battery-operated fairy lights as a spooky ornament for your front door at Halloween.

MATERIALS

- 75–100 pine cones
- 30cm straw wreath
- Twenty-four small wired toadstools
- White paint (chalk paint or emulsion both work well)
- Maldon salt
- Cardboard tubes or empty loo rolls, cut into 4cm sections
- An old toothbrush
- Hot glue gun
- Spray adhesive
- Wire

1. Clean your pine cones. Brush off any obvious debris or unwelcome tiny visitors, and wash and dry if necessary.

2. Snap any stalks off the bottom of the cones, as this will give you a better surface for gluing.

3. Cut a 10cm length of wire and fold into a U-shape, then twist together about half way down. Bend the two legs out at right angles, then glue from the twist down onto the back of the straw form to make your hanging loop.

4. Paint the wreath white, just so no jarring gaps of colour peep through your finished design.

5. Cut your cardboard tubes into little sections, roughly 3cm wide. These will act as little stands to keep your cones upright while the paint dries.

6. Thin your white paint with an equal volume of water so it reaches the consistency of single cream. It should be wet enough to adhere to the pine cones, but still have a touch of thickness so that it will remain opaque.

7. Dip your toothbrush in the paint, and use it to brush the tips of the pine cone white, leaving the centre unpainted.

8. Stand the cone in your loo roll tube to dry, and repeat until you have painted all 100. They will dry quite quickly as the cones are so porous.

9. At this point I would suggest sorting your cones in to three groups of small, medium and large. Starting on the inside of the straw ring, add a generous layer of hot glue to the base of the smaller pines cones and attach them to the form, pressing firmly until the adhesive has solidified.

10. Once you have the inside ring completed, begin to glue on the larger cones to the outside, tucking in the medium ones to fill any gaps until the whole wreath has been covered.

11. Working a small section at a time, hold the spray adhesive about 30cm away from the wreath and give it a healthy blast of glue. Working quickly, sprinkle on some Maldon salt, and then repeat until the whole form is covered; it has a lovely effect on both plain and painted cones.

12. Shake off the excess salt.

13. Take one of the little toadstools and fold the wire in half to give you a U-shape. Apply some hot glue to the base of the toadstool then push the wire down in between the gaps in the pine cones to secure them.

14. Repeat with the other toadstools, then tidy up any threads of glue.

QUICK PINE CONE CANDLE RING

MATERIALS

- Five pine cones
- Hot glue gun

1. Turn your pine cones upside down and arrange them in a circle, ensuring the hole will be big enough for your candle.

2. Push the pine cones together gently so that the layers slot into each other slightly. This will help keep them together long enough for you to glue them.

3. Add a blob of glue at the five points where the pine cones intersect, and once the first blobs have dried, add an extra squirt just to be on the safe side (you don't want to apply a huge amount all at once or the liquid adhesive will drip down between the cones and be visible).

4. Turn upside down and place over your candle. Do not leave unattended when lit, and do not let it burn down too low as the pine cones are flammable.

CHAPTER ELEVEN

WILD WILLOW WINTER WREATH WITH CINNAMON AND DRIED ORANGE

NOTHING EMBODIES THE promise of Christmas like the fragrance of orange and spice, and this beautiful wreath will fill your home with a wonderful festive scent. One of my favourite traditions is the week before Christmas when we all gather in my friend's barn to make our front door wreaths. Drinking mulled wine and surrounded by candlelight, with swathes of cut and foraged greenery piled up along trestle tables, we start by making basic willow rings and then get creative. The tradition of bringing greenery into the home during the winter dates back millennia; the Romans used to decorate with evergreens as part of Saturnalia, their mid-winter festival, and Germanic tribes would carry green boughs indoors to celebrate the winter solstice. Ivy symbolises friendship and love, holly offers protection, and pine denotes life, making this wreath the perfect gift for friends or family.

The wreath shown here has a loose, unstructured design for a contemporary feel, and would look beautiful hanging on a door or painted dresser. It is best made fresh on the day you are going to decorate it, as the willow will be flexible enough for you to twist the greenery in between the withies to hold them in place. It is possible to buy dried orange slices from floristry supply shops, but I like to make my own as not only is it cheap and easy to do, but the warm citrus fragrance will fill your home whilst they are drying. They are so

easy to make and will last for ages if kept dry, so why not make extra while you have the oven on? Thread a little baker's twine through each slice to make a pretty Christmas tree decoration or to make gift wrapping look extra special.

You can also use the slices as a flavouring in tea or water, or as a stylish addition to cakes or snack platters. They taste delicious (if chewy) when dipped in dark chocolate, and would be a welcome gift, packed in a Kilner jar and tied with festive ribbon. Slice the oranges to about 5mm thick, carefully removing any seeds. Dry as usual, then dip into good quality dark chocolate and leave to set on baking parchment; sprinkle with a little sea salt for an extra burst of flavour. Consume within a week of drying.

MATERIALS

- Nine or ten willow withies, as thick as your little finger and around 70cm long; cutting them in winter for wreath-making is ideal, as you won't need to strip the leaves off. If it is very cold outside when they are harvested it is a good idea to bring them indoors a few hours before you intend to use them, as it will make them more malleable and less prone to snapping.
- 6–8 lengths of foraged ivy
- Pine sprigs
- Bunch of holly, with berries if possible. (If you can't find fresh holly, rosehips and hawthorn berries also look fabulous. Faux berries are readily available at craft shops).
- 1m of red Christmas ribbon, 1cm wide
- 1.5m of red ribbon, 2.5cm wide
- Nine cinnamon sticks
- Two oranges
- Floristry wire
- Secateurs
- Glue gun and glue sticks

1. Preheat the oven to a low temperature of about 120 degrees, then cut the oranges into slices about a centimetre thick.

2. Gently pat dry with kitchen paper and place them on a wire rack over a baking tray, before popping them in the oven for about three hours until they are dry. Keep an eye on them and turn occasionally to stop any scorching, as they can catch quite easily. Thinner slices

will obviously dry more quickly, so might need taking out before the thicker ones.

3. Next, using the hot glue gun, apply a couple of blobs of adhesive to the cinnamon sticks and glue into bundles of three.

4. Taking a 20cm length of wire, wrap twice around the centre of each bundle and twist the two together, leaving you two long tails to tie the bundle on to the wreath.

5. Cut the narrower Christmas ribbon into three vaguely equal sections, then wrap a piece two or three times around each bundle to cover the wire, finishing with a bow and ensuring that the wire tails are free.

6. Take a piece of willow and, using your thumbs, bend it all the way along to warm the wood up a little. Now form it into a circle roughly 35–40cm in diameter, and tuck either end through the hoop you have made, wrapping each tip back around the hoop as many times as you can.

7. Using your next piece of willow, insert the blunt end into the hoop until roughly half its length is poking through, then continue to wrap either end of the withy in and out of the circle. Repeat until you have used all the willow, then gently push the wreath into a circle shape. Snip off any obvious ends with the secateurs.

8. Taking the evergreen sprigs, snip them into little pieces about 10cm long. Tie the reel wire on to the wreath and wrap it around the sprig to securely it firmly on to the base.

9. Lay each new sprig over the base of the last one so they roughly overlap, and continue to repeat until the whole form is covered.

10. Attach the ivy with wire, tucking the ends in between the willow to secure. (If the ivy stem is quite thick, it can be covered by wiring on a few more evergreen sprigs.)

11. By this point you should have a lovely fat base to work on, so

the holly stems can just be trimmed and pushed into the greenery and withies where they will tuck in nicely. Space any sprigs with berries out so they are spread evenly around the ring.

12. Cut a 20cm length of wire and push 10cm through the orange slice just inside the rind, before folding in half and securing with a couple of twists. Repeat this process until you have ten slices in total.

13. Using the two ends of the wire, tie the oranges onto the wreath in pairs, fanning them out as you go, then add the cinnamon bundles.

14. Cut the wider red ribbon in two. Fold one piece in half and, starting front to back, pass the fold through the ring at the top, before pulling the two ends through the loop you have just made. Tie in a knot at the ends to make a hanging loop, then finish by tying a bow around the bottom of the hanger if you like.

CHAPTER TWELVE

JULESTJERNE WREATH

JULESTJERNER, OR DANISH paper woven stars, are one of the most iconic of Scandinavian Christmas ornaments, and are very easy to make when you have got the knack. Once you have made this wreath, surplus stars look wonderful piled up in bowls with a few fairy lights, strewn across your Christmas table, hung on the tree or strung together to make an attractive mobile. We hang a branch from the ceiling and suspend the stars and a few fairy lights from the twigs for an alternative rustic decoration.

My Danish grandmother taught me to make julestjerner when I was little. Although you can buy ready-made packs of strips, it is easy to make your own; use leftover rolls of wallpaper, old newspapers or sheet music to give the necessary length. (You can even make them from curling ribbon if your eyesight is up to it). The only caveat is that the strips need to be absolutely straight in order to weave them successfully, so I would suggest using a paper guillotine to cut them (fold the paper in half lengthways before you cut it to make it easier). Give the paper a quick iron if necessary so it will lie nice and flat. The rule of thumb is that the length of the strip needs to be thirty times the width, so a 1.5cm wide strip will need to be 45cm long; this will give you a star just over four times the width, about 6.5cm across. If you are struggling to get the paper to slip through the holes, you might find it easier if you cut the end of the strips off at an angle; this makes it much easier to push it through the tight gaps.

MATERIALS

- Eight stars, made from thirty-two strips of paper measuring 1.5cm x 45cm (or buy them online)
- Scissors
- Hot glue gun

1. Fold your strips in half lengthways.

2. To make the first star, take four strips and alternately weave them inside and outside the adjacent strip to form a square.

3. Pull the strips so the square closes up.

4. Lay your strips out so one is pointing up at the left-hand side. Fold this down, then repeat with the other three strips.

5. Take the fourth strip and tuck it into the hole made by the first strip.

6. Take the top right strip and bend it away from you, folding it into a triangle.

7. Now bend the strip towards you, up and away from you and back down through the hole by the triangle,

then pull it tight so it makes a three-dimensional point. This is probably the most difficult manoeuvre of the project, but once you have mastered it successfully the rest of the star will be a breeze.

8. Keep turning the star 90 degrees to the right and repeating this fold until all the right-hand strips have been used.

9. Turn the star over and repeat until all the (new) right-hand strips have been folded. You should now have eight external points on your star.

10. Now we are going to make the internal points (the working ends of your strips should now have moved to the centre).

11. Using the bottom right-hand strip, lift it up, then twist down and to the right, to make a triangle.

12. Moving the working strip above it out of the way, take the end and loop it up and over, pushing it through the adjacent hole. The tip should come out of the top star point to the left. Pull gently until it forms a point.

13. Repeat with the other three strips until you have four points.

14. Turn the star over and repeat with the last four strips to make four more points.

15. Snip off the excess working length where it comes through the external points.

16. Repeat to make eight stars in total.

17. To make a wreath, lay the stars out on your working surface. You will see that if you turn the stars there are differences in the gaps between the points. Pinch the two points of one of the smaller sections to flatten them slightly, then slide them in between those of a larger section, pushing the tips into the gap in the middle of the triangles so they slot together. Fix in place with a blob of glue, and repeat to make four double stars.

18. Once again slide the tips of the smaller points in between those of the bigger ones, this time at an angle, so you form a round shape.

19. Continue sliding in the stars and securing with a blob of glue until the wreath is complete.

FABRIC BIRD TEMPLATE FOR EASTER WREATH

SUPPLIERS

Creativ Company Ltd.
www.cc-craft.co.uk
Floristry supplies, tools, straw
wreaths, air dry clay, glue,
acrylic paint, ribbon

Hygge Style
www.hyggestyle.co.uk
0800 012 4116
Straw and willow wreaths,
wooden houses, Scandinavian
ribbons, paper star strips

Country Baskets
www.countrybaskets.co.uk
Floristry supplies, wire and
natural bases

Musgrove Willows
Willow Fields,
Lakewall,
Westonzoyland,
Bridgwater,
Somerset
TA7 0LP
01278 691105
www.musgrovewillows.co.uk
Willow withy bundles,
workshops and kits

Castle Farm Kent
Castle Farm
Redmans Lane,
Shoreham,
Sevenoaks,
Kent
TN14 7UB
01959 523219
www.castlefarmkent.co.uk
Fresh and dried lavender
bunches, wreath kits and
essential oils. Also picnics in
lavender fields.

Coates English Willow
www.coatesenglishwillow.co.uk
Fresh and dried willow, visitor
centre and cafe, basketry kits
and workshops.

The Flower Shop, Pulborough
56 Lower St,
Pulborough,
West Sussex,
RH20 2BW
01798 875488
www.theflowershop-
pulborough.co.uk
Country village florist with an
emphasis on sustainability